Social Studies

Level 3

Thank You!

Thank you for purchasing this workbook.

I hope it will benefit your student!

If you like this . . .

Please leave a 5-star review and check out more writing resources:

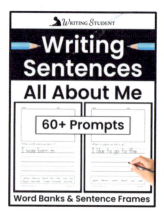 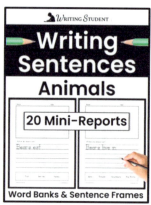 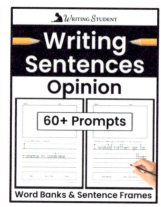 

Contact

Writing Student™ materials are created by Angela Dansie
Email: https://writingstudent.com/pages/contact
Website: https://writingstudent.com

Social Studies
Level 3 Workbook

Table of Contents

Civics: American Symbols . . . . pg. 5

American Flag, Bald Eagle, Liberty Bell, Lincoln Memorial,
Mount Rushmore, Pledge of Allegiance, Statue of Liberty,
The Great Seal, The Star-Spangled Banner,
The White House, The Washington Monument

Economics: Transportation . . . . pg. 29

Airplane, Bus, Ship, Subway, Train, Truck

History: U.S. Holidays . . . . pg. 43

New Year's Day, Martin Luther King Jr. Day, President's Day,
Memorial Day, Juneteenth, Independence Day, Labor Day,
Columbus Day, Veteran's Day, Thanksgiving Day,
Christmas Day

Geography: Landforms & Habitats . . . . pg. 67

Arctic, Bay, Canyon, Cave, City, Coast/Beach, Desert, Dunes,
Forest, Freshwater, Glacier, Grassland, Hill, Island, Mountain,
Ocean, Peninsula, Plain, Plateau, Rainforest, River, Valley,
Volcano, Wetland

Social Studies
Workbook

Name _____

Civics:

American Symbols

American Flag

- The colors of the flag are red, white, and blue.
- Red stands for bravery.
- White stands for purity.
- Blue stands for justice.
- The flag has 13 stripes.
- The stripes stand for the 13 original colonies.
- The flag has 50 stars.
- Each star represents a state in the United States.
- The flag is sometimes called the "Stars and Stripes".
- The first American flag was made in 1777 by Betsy Ross.
- We display the American flag on national holidays.

Write 4 facts you have learned.

American Flag

1. _____

   _____

2. _____

   _____

3. _____

   _____

4. _____

   _____

Bald Eagle

- The bald eagle is the national bird of the United States.
- It was chosen as the national bird in 1782.
- Bald eagles are not really bald, they have white feathers on their heads.
- They have yellow beaks and sharp talons.
- Bald eagles live near rivers, lakes, and coastal regions.
- They mainly eat fish, but also hunt small animals.
- Bald eagles build large nests called eyries in tall trees.
- Their wingspan can be over 7 feet wide.
- The bald eagle symbolizes freedom and strength.
- You can find bald eagles on the Great Seal.

Write 4 facts you have learned.

Bald Eagle

1. _____

_____

2. _____

_____

3. _____

_____

4. _____

_____

Liberty Bell

- The Liberty Bell is symbol of American independence and freedom.

- The bell was made in 1752 out of copper and tin.

- It has the words "Proclaim Liberty Throughout All the Land".

- It was used to call people to important meetings and events.

- It was run on July 8, 1776, to mark the first public reading of the Declaration of Independence.

- The Liberty Bell has a big crack in it.

- The crack happened the first time it was rung.

- You can visit it at the Liberty Bell Center.

- It is located in Philadelphia, Pennsylvania.

Name

Write 4 facts you have learned.

Liberty Bell

1. _____

_____

2. _____

_____

3. _____

_____

4. _____

_____

Lincoln Memorial

- The Lincoln Memorial is in Washington, D.C.
- It honors Abraham Lincoln, the 16th President of the U.S.A.
- The memorial was dedicated in 1922.
- It looks like a Greek temple with 36 columns.
- Inside, there is a large statue of Abraham Lincoln sitting in a chair.
- The statue is 19 feet tall.
- The words of the Gettysburg Address are engraved on the wall.
- The Lincoln Memorial is a symbol of freedom and unity.
- Many important events, like Martin Luther King Jr.'s "I Have a Dream" speech, happened here.

Write 4 facts you have learned.

Lincoln Memorial

1. _____

_____

2. _____

_____

3. _____

_____

4. _____

_____

Mount Rushmore

- Mount Rushmore is in South Dakota.
- It has the faces of four U.S. Presidents carved into it.
- The presidents are George Washington, Thomas Jefferson, Theodore Roosevelt, and Abraham Lincoln.
- The monument was completed in 1941.
- The faces are carved into a granite mountain.
- Each face is about 60 feet tall.
- It was designed by sculptor Gutzon Borglum.
- The project took 14 years to finish.
- Mount Rushmore is a symbol of American history and leadership.
- Millions of people visit every year to see the carvings.

Name _____   Date _____

Write 4 facts you have learned.

Mount Rushmore

1. _____

    _____

2. _____

    _____

3. _____

    _____

4. _____

    _____

Pledge of Allegiance

- The Pledge of Allegiance is a promise of loyalty to the United States.
- It was written by Francis Bellamy in 1892.
- The Pledge is often recited at the start of school days and public events.
- People usually stand and place their right hand over their heart while reciting it.
- The Pledge of Allegiance is a way to show respect for the country. It is a symbol of patriotism and national pride.
- The words of the Pledge are: "I pledge allegiance to the Flag of the United States of America, and to the Republic for which it stands, one Nation under God, indivisible, with liberty and justice for all."

Write 4 facts you have learned.

Pledge of Allegiance

1. _____

   _____

2. _____

   _____

3. _____

   _____

4. _____

   _____

Statue of Liberty

- The Statue of Liberty is in New York Harbor.
- It was a gift from France to the United States in 1886.
- The Statue of Liberty is a symbol of hope and welcome for immigrants arriving by sea.
- Lady Liberty holds a torch in her right hand.
- In her left hand, she holds a tablet with the date July 4, 1776 written on it.
- The statue is made of copper and has turned green over time.
- The full name is "Liberty Enlightening the World".
- The statue is 151 feet tall from base to torch.
- People can visit and climb up to the crown for a view of the harbor.

Write 4 facts you have learned.

Statue of Liberty

1. _____

_____

2. _____

_____

3. _____

_____

4. _____

_____

The Great Seal

- The Great Seal is the official emblem of the United States.
- The seal shows a bald eagle holding an olive branch and arrows.
- The olive branch stands for peace.
- The arrows stand for war.
- Above the eagle's head is a circle of 13 stars.
- The stars represent the original 13 colonies.
- The eagle holds a banner in its beak that says "E Pluribus Unum."
- "E Pluribus Unum" means "Out of many, one."
- The Great Seal is used on important documents and official papers. It is on the one-dollar bill.
- It is a symbol of the nation's unity and strength.

Write 4 facts you have learned.

The Great Seal

1. _____

_____

2. _____

_____

3. _____

_____

4. _____

_____

The Star-Spangled Banner

- "The Star-Spangled Banner" is the national anthem of the United States.
- It was written by Francis Scott Key in 1814.
- He write the song after seeing the American flag still flying after a battle during the War of 1812.
- The song's lyrics describe the flag and the battle at Fort McHenry. The anthem has four verses.
- The song starts with the words, "O say can you see, by the dawn's early light."
- People often stand and place their hand over their heart while the anthem is played.
- It is a symbol of American resilience and patriotism.

Write 4 facts you have learned.

The Star-Spangled Banner

1. _____

   _____

2. _____

   _____

3. _____

   _____

4. _____

   _____

The White House

- The White House is in Washington, D.C.
- It is the home and office of the President of the United States.
- The White House was built in 1792.
- John Adams was the first president to live in it.
- The building has 132 rooms.
- It is made of white-painted sandstone.
- The White House has a famous oval-shaped room called the Oval Office.
- Important meetings and events happen at the White House.
- The address of the White House is 1600 Pennsylvania Ave.
- It is a symbol of the American presidency and government.

Write 4 facts you have learned.

The White House

1. _____

_____

2. _____

_____

3. _____

_____

4. _____

_____

Washington Monument

- The Washington Monument is in Washington, D.C.
- It honors George Washington, the first President of the United States.
- The monument is an obelisk, a tall, four-sided pillar.
- It is made of marble, granite, and bluestone gneiss.
- The construction started in 1848 and finished in 1884.
- The monument is 555 feet tall.
- It is the tallest stone structure in the world.
- There are 897 steps inside, but visitors usually take an elevator to the top.
- The Washington Monument is a symbol of respect and admiration for George Washington.

Name

Date

Write 4 facts you have learned.

The Washington Monument

1. _____

_____

2. _____

_____

3. _____

_____

4. _____

_____

Economics:

Transportation

Airplane

- Airplanes are a fast way to travel long distances.
- They can fly high in the sky, above the clouds.
- The Wright brothers made the first successful airplane flight in 1903.
- Airplanes have wings, a tail, and engines to help them fly.
- They take off from and land on runways at airports.
- Passengers sit in seats inside the airplane during the flight.
- Pilots use controls in the cockpit to fly the airplane.
- Airplanes can carry people and cargo to different places around the world.

Write 4 facts you have learned.

Airplane

1. _____

   _____

2. _____

   _____

3. _____

   _____

4. _____

   _____

Bus

- Buses are large vehicles that carry many passengers.
- They travel on roads and have fixed routes and schedules.
- People use buses to get to work, school, and other places.
- They stop at bus stops to pick up and drop off passengers.
- School buses are yellow and take children to and from school.
- Buses can be powered by gasoline, diesel, electricity, or natural gas.
- Riding the bus can help reduce traffic and pollution.
- Buses provide an affordable way for people to travel within a city or town.

Write 4 facts you have learned.

Bus

1. _____

_____

2. _____

_____

3. _____

_____

4. _____

_____

Ship

- Ships are large boats that travel on water.
- They are used to transport people and goods across oceans, seas, and rivers.
- Ships can be powered by engines, sails, or both.
- Cargo ships carry goods like cars, food, and clothing.
- Passenger ships, like cruise ships, carry people on vacations.
- Military ships are used by navies to protect countries.
- Ships have been used for thousands of years for exploration and trade.
- Ports are places where ships load and unload goods.

Write 4 facts you have learned.

Ship

1. _____

_____

2. _____

_____

3. _____

_____

4. _____

_____

Subway

- Subways are underground trains that carry passengers in cities.

- They travel through tunnels beneath the streets.

- Subways have many cars linked together, forming a train.

- They stop at stations where passengers get on and off.

- Subways are powered by electricity.

- They help reduce traffic congestion in busy cities.

- Subways run on fixed routes and schedules.

- Many large cities, like New York and London, have subway systems.

- Riding the subway is faster than driving in crowded areas.

Write 4 facts you have learned.

Subway

1. _____

   _____

2. _____

   _____

3. _____

   _____

4. _____

   _____

Train

- Trains run on tracks and can carry passengers or cargo.
- They have an engine and multiple cars linked together.
- Trains can be powered by diesel, electricity, or steam.
- Passenger trains take people between cities and across countries.
- High-speed trains can travel very fast, sometimes over 200 miles per hour.
- Trains stop at stations where passengers can board them.
- Freight trains carry goods like coal, grain, and lumber.
- They are an efficient way to transport large amounts of goods.

Write 4 facts you have learned.

Train

1. _____

_____

2. _____

_____

3. _____

_____

4. _____

_____

Truck

- Trucks are large vehicles used to transport goods on roads.

- they have powerful engines to carry heavy loads.

- Delivery trucks bring packages to homes and businesses.

- Semi-trucks haul cargo over long distances.

- Trucks can carry many types of goods, like food, furniture, and machinery.

- They often deliver goods from factories to stores.

- Some trucks are refrigerated, to carry perishable items.

- Trucks help keep stores stocked with the products people need.

Write 4 facts you have learned.

Truck

1. _____

_____

2. _____

_____

3. _____

_____

4. _____

_____

History:

Holidays

New Year's Day

- New Year's Day is celebrated on January 1st each year.

- It marks the beginning of the new year on our calendar.

- People often stay up late on New Year's Eve to celebrate the arrival of the new year.

- Families have parties and watch fireworks to celebrate.

- Traditional foods, like black-eyed peas and cabbage, are eaten for good luck.

- The Times Square Ball Drop at midnight in New York City is a famous New Year's Eve event.

- Many people make New Year's resolutions and set goals for the upcoming year.

Name _____ Date _____

Write 4 facts you have learned.

New Year's Day

1. _____

   _____

2. _____

   _____

3. _____

   _____

4. _____

   _____

Martin Luther King Jr. Day

- Martin Luther King Jr. Day is a national holiday in the United States.
- It is celebrated on the third Monday in January.
- The holiday honors Dr. Martin Luther King Jr., a leader in the Civil Rights Movement.
- Dr. King was born on January 15, 1929.
- He is famous for his "I Have a Dream" speech and his work to end racial segregation.
- Many people celebrate by participating in community service and volunteer activities.
- Dr. King's work for equality and justice is remembered.

Write 4 facts you have learned.

Martin Luther King Jr. Day

1. _____

_____

2. _____

_____

3. _____

_____

4. _____

_____

President's Day

- President's Day is a national holiday in the United States.

- It is celebrated on the third Monday in February.

- The holiday honors all U.S. Presidents, especially George Washington and Abraham Lincoln.

- George Washington was born on February 22, and Abraham Lincoln on February 12.

- It is a day for remembering the contributions of all Presidents to the country.

- Some people celebrate by learning about American history and Presidents.

Name _____   Date _____

Write 4 facts you have learned.

President's Day

1. _____

   _____

2. _____

   _____

3. _____

   _____

4. _____

   _____

Memorial Day

- Memorial Day is a national holiday in the United States.
- It is celebrated on the last Monday in May.
- The holiday honors soldiers who died while serving in the military.
- Memorial Day was originally called Decoration Day.
- People often visit cemeteries and place flags or flowers on graves.
- Many communities hold parades and ceremonies to remember fallen soldiers.
- Families and friends often gather for picnics and barbecues.
- The holiday began after the Civil War in the 1860s.
- On Memorial Day, the American flag is flown at half-staff until noon.

Write 4 facts you have learned.

Memorial Day

1. _____

   _____

2. _____

   _____

3. _____

   _____

4. _____

   _____

Juneteenth

- Juneteenth is a holiday celebrating the end of slavery in the United States.

- It is observed on June 19th each year.

- The holiday marks the day in 1865 when enslaved people in Texas learned they were free.

- This happened more than two years after the Emancipation Proclamation was signed.

- Juneteenth is also known as Freedom Day or Emancipation Day.

- People celebrate with parades, picnics, and family gatherings.

Write 4 facts you have learned.

Juneteenth

1. _____

_____

2. _____

_____

3. _____

_____

4. _____

_____

53

Independence Day

- Independence Day is celebrated on July 4th every year.
- The holiday marks the adoption of the Declaration of Independence in 1776.
- On this day, the American colonies declared their independence from Britain.
- The Fourth of July is the "birthday" of the United States as a new country.
- People celebrate with fireworks, parades, picnics and barbecues.
- Many people wear red, white, and blue clothes and display American flags outside their homes.

Write 4 facts you have learned.

Independence Day

1. _____

_____

2. _____

_____

3. _____

_____

4. _____

_____

55

Labor Day

- Labor Day is a national holiday in the United States.

- It is celebrated on the first Monday in September.

- The holiday honors the contributions and achievements of American workers.

- Labor Day was first celebrated in 1882 in New York City.

- Most workers enjoy the day off.

- Many people enjoy a long weekend and celebrate with barbecues, picnics, and outdoor activities.

- Labor Day marks the unofficial end of summer.

Write 4 facts you have learned.

Labor Day

1. _____

_____

2. _____

_____

3. _____

_____

4. _____

_____

Columbus Day

- Columbus Day is a national holiday in the United States.

- It is celebrated on the second Monday in October.

- The holiday honors Christopher Columbus's arrival in the Americas on October 12, 1492.

- Columbus was an Italian explorer sponsored by Spain.

- Columbus had three ships on his first voyage: the Nina, the Pinta, and the Santa Maria.

- The holiday is a time to learn about Columbus's voyages and their impact on history.

- Some people observe Indigenous Peoples' Day instead, to honor Native American cultures.

Write 4 facts you have learned.

Columbus Day

1. _____

   _____

2. _____

   _____

3. _____

   _____

4. _____

   _____

Veteran's Day

- Veteran's Day is a national holiday in the United States.

- It is celebrated on November 11 each year.

- The holiday honors all military veterans who have served in the U.S. Armed Forces.

- Veteran's Day was originally called Armistice Day.

- November 11 marks the end of World War I in 1918.

- People often thank veterans for their service on this day.

- Many communities hold parades and meetings to remember the sacrifices and contributions of veterans.

- Veteran's Day is different from Memorial Day, which honors those who died in service.

Write 4 facts you have learned.

Veteran's Day

1. _____

_____

2. _____

_____

3. _____

_____

4. _____

_____

Thanksgiving

- Thanksgiving is a national holiday in the United States.
- It is celebrated on the fourth Thursday in November.
- The first Thanksgiving in 1621 was a three-day feast attended by both Pilgrims and Native Americans.
- The Native Americans who helped the Pilgrims survive were from the Wamponoag tribe.
- Squanto, a member of the tribe, acted as an interpreter and taught the Pilgrims how to plant corn and to fish.
- The first Thanksgiving is a symbol of friendship and cooperation between different cultures.
- Thanksgiving is a time to express gratitude and to help those in need.

Name   Date

Write 4 facts you have learned.

Thanksgiving Day

1. _____

    _____

2. _____

    _____

3. _____

    _____

4. _____

    _____

Christmas

- Christmas is celebrated on December 25th each year.

- It is a holiday that celebrates the birth of Jesus Christ.

- People decorate their homes with Christmas trees, lights, and ornaments.

- Many families give gifts and cards during Christmas.

- Christmas carols and holiday songs are sung to celebrate.

- Christmas is a time for family gatherings and meals.

- The holiday season includes customs and traditions from around the world.

- Santa Claus brings gifts to children on Christmas Eve.

Write 4 facts you have learned.

Christmas Day

1. _____

_____

2. _____

_____

3. _____

_____

4. _____

_____

Geography:

Landforms

and Habitats

Arctic

- The Arctic is a polar region at the northernmost part of the Earth.

- It is extremely cold. The land is covered in snow and ice.

- The Arctic tundra has no trees. The frozen ground is called permafrost.

- Sea ice covers much of the Arctic Ocean, especially in winter.

- Animals like polar bears, Arctic foxes, and seals live there.

- Indigenous peoples, such as the Inuit, live in the Arctic.

- During the summer, it has 24-hour daylight. In winter, the sun doesn't come up.

- The Arctic is rich in natural resources like oil, gas, and minerals.

Write 4 facts you have learned.

Arctic

1. _____

   _____

2. _____

   _____

3. _____

   _____

4. _____

   _____

Bay

- A bay is a body of water that is partly surrounded by land.

- They often have calm waters because they are protected from strong waves.

- Bays can be good places for boats to dock.

- Bays are often found where rivers meet the sea.

- Many animals, like fish and birds, live in and around bays.

- Bays are great spots for fishing, swimming, and boating.

- Some famous bays are the San Francisco Bay and the Chesapeake Bay.

Write 4 facts you have learned.

Bay

1. _____

   _____

2. _____

   _____

3. _____

   _____

4. _____

   _____

Canyon

- Canyons are deep valleys with steep sides.
- They are often formed by rivers cutting through rock over a long time.
- The Grand Canyon in Arizona is one of the most famous canyons.
- Canyons can be very wide and deep.
- Many animals, like eagles and lizards, live in canyons.
- People visit canyons to hike, camp, and take pictures.
- Canyons have layers of rock that show Earth's history.
- Canyons are beautiful places with amazing views.

Write 4 facts you have learned.

Canyon

1. _____

   _____

2. _____

   _____

3. _____

   _____

4. _____

   _____

Cave

- A cave is a large hole or space inside a hill or mountain.
- Caves can be dark and cool inside.
- They are often formed by water wearing away rock over many years.
- Many animals, like bats and bears, live in caves.
- Some caves have beautiful formations called stalactites and stalagmites.
- People explore caves to discover interesting rocks and hidden spaces.
- Some caves have ancient drawings made by early humans.
- Caves can have underground rivers and lakes.

Write 4 facts you have learned.

Cave

1. _____

_____

2. _____

_____

3. _____

_____

4. _____

_____

City

- Cities are places where many people live and work.
- Tall buildings called skyscrapers are in big cities.
- Cities have busy streets with lots of traffic and people.
- Cities have lots of cars, buses, and trains for transportation.
- People live in apartments or houses close together.
- Cities have many shops, restaurants, and schools.
- Parks in cities give people places to play and relax.
- Many jobs and businesses are found in cities.
- Cities have museums, theaters, and sports stadiums.
- Cities are exciting places with many different things to see and do.

Write 4 facts you have learned.

City

1. _____

_____

2. _____

_____

3. _____

_____

4. _____

_____

Coast / Beach

- The coast is where the land meets the ocean.
- Beaches are sandy or rocky areas along the coast.
- Waves crash onto the shore at the beach.
- Seagulls, crabs, starfish, sand dollars, and pelicans are common animals found at the beach.
- Some beaches have tide pools with small sea creatures.
- Sand dunes are hills of sand found at some beaches.
- Many people visit beaches to swim, play, and relax.
- Beachcombing is fun for finding shells and other treasures.
- Lighthouses help ships sail safely near the coast.

Write 4 facts you have learned.

Coast / Beach

1. _____

   _____

2. _____

   _____

3. _____

   _____

4. _____

   _____

Desert

- Deserts are very dry places with little rain.
- Some deserts are hot, like the Sahara, and some are cold, like the Gobi Desert.
- Deserts can be very hot during the day and very cold at night.
- The soil in deserts is usually sandy or rocky.
- Cacti and other unique plants grow in deserts because they can live with little water.
- Animals like camels, lizards, and scorpions live in deserts.
- Deserts cover a big part of the Earth.
- People in deserts save water carefully because it is so scarce.

Write 4 facts you have learned.

Desert

1. _____

   _____

2. _____

   _____

3. _____

   _____

4. _____

   _____

Dunes

- Dunes are hills of sand found in deserts and on beaches.

- They are formed by the wind blowing sand into piles.

- Dunes can change shape and move over time because of the wind.

- Plants like grasses can grow on dunes and help hold the sand in place.

- Animals like lizards and beetles live in and around dunes.

- Some dunes are very tall and can be as high as mountains.

- The Sahara Desert has many large sand dunes.

- People enjoy climbing and exploring dunes for fun.

Write 4 facts you have learned.

Dunes

1. _____

_____

2. _____

_____

3. _____

_____

4. _____

_____

Forest

- Forests are areas with lots of trees.

- Many animals, like deer, birds, and bears, live in forests.

- Forests can be found all over the world.

- Trees in forests give us oxygen to breathe.

- Forests have different layers: the canopy, understory, and forest floor.

- Evergreen forests have trees that stay green all year.

- Deciduous forests have trees that lose their leaves in the fall.

- People get wood and paper from forests.

Write 4 facts you have learned.

Forest

1. _____

   _____

2. _____

   _____

3. _____

   _____

4. _____

   _____

Freshwater

- Freshwater is water that is not salty.
- Lakes, rivers, and ponds are examples of freshwater.
- Fish, frogs, and ducks live in freshwater habitats.
- Freshwater is important for plants and animals to survive.
- Many cities get their water from freshwater lakes and rivers.
- People use freshwater for drinking, cooking, and cleaning.
- Wetlands, like marshes and swamps, are also freshwater habitats.
- We need to keep freshwater clean to stay healthy and protect wildlife.

Write 4 facts you have learned.

Freshwater

1. _____

    _____

2. _____

    _____

3. _____

    _____

4. _____

    _____

Glacier

- A glacier is a large, slow-moving river of ice.
- Glaciers form in places where it is very cold, like the Arctic and mountains.
- They are made of layers of snow that have been pressed into ice over many years.
- Glaciers can be very big, sometimes covering whole mountains.
- As glaciers move, they can shape the land by carving out valleys and lakes.
- Many animals, like polar bears and seals, live near glaciers.
- Glaciers melt in the summer and can create rivers and streams.
- Some famous glaciers are in Alaska, Antarctica, and the Himalayas.

Write 4 facts you have learned.

Glacier

1. _____

_____

2. _____

_____

3. _____

_____

4. _____

_____

Grassland

- Grasslands are large open areas covered mostly with grass.
- They are found on every continent except Antarctica.
- Grasslands can be called prairies, savannas, or steppes.
- Many animals, like bison, zebras, lions, elephants, giraffes, cheetahs, and kangaroos live in grasslands.
- Grasslands have few trees and lots of wide, open spaces.
- They often have rich soil that is good for farming.
- Grasslands can be very dry or have lots of rain.
- People use grasslands to raise cattle and grow crops.

Write 4 facts you have learned.

Grassland

1. _____

_____

2. _____

_____

3. _____

_____

4. _____

_____

Hill

- Hills are raised areas of land, not as tall as mountains.

- They are usually round and gentle in shape.

- Many animals, like rabbits and deer, live on hills.

- Hills are often covered with grass, bushes, and trees.

- Hills can be found all around the world.

- Some hills are made by nature, and some are made by people.

- Hills can be good places for farming and grazing animals.

- People can walk or hike up hills for fun.

- The tops of hills are called hilltops.

Write 4 facts you have learned.

Hill

1. _____

   _____

2. _____

   _____

3. _____

   _____

4. _____

   _____

93

Island

- An island is a piece of land surrounded by water.

- Islands can be found in oceans, seas, rivers, and lakes.

- Some islands are big, like Hawaii, and some are small.

- Many animals, like birds and turtles, live on islands.

- Islands often have beautiful beaches and forests.

- People visit islands for fun activities like swimming and hiking.

- Some islands are made by volcanoes erupting.

- Coral reefs can form around islands in warm oceans.

- Islands can be connected to the mainland by bridges or boats.

Name   Date

Write 4 facts you have learned.

Island

1. _____

   _____

2. _____

   _____

3. _____

   _____

4. _____

   _____

Mountain

- Mountains are tall, rocky places that rise high above the land.

- Some mountains are covered with snow on top.

- Many animals, like goats, bears, mountain lions, bighorn sheep, and eagles, live on mountains.

- Trees and plants can grow on mountains, but the tops can be too cold.

- People like to hike and climb mountains for fun.

- The tallest mountain in the world is Mount Everest.

- Mountains can be part of big ranges, like the Rocky Mountains, the Andes, and the Alps.

- Rivers and streams often start in the mountains.

- Mountains are formed by movements of the Earth's crust.

Write 4 facts you have learned.

Mountain

1. _____

   _____

2. _____

   _____

3. _____

   _____

4. _____

   _____

Ocean

- Oceans are large bodies of salty water that cover most of the Earth's surface.
- There are five oceans: the Pacific, Atlantic, Indian, Southern, and Arctic.
- Oceans are home to many animals like whales, dolphins, and sharks.
- Coral reefs in the ocean are like underwater cities full of colorful fish.
- Oceans provide food, like fish and seaweed, for people around the world.
- The ocean helps regulate the Earth's climate by storing heat.
- The deepest part of the ocean is called the Mariana Trench.

Write 4 facts you have learned.

Ocean

1. _____

_____

2. _____

_____

3. _____

_____

4. _____

_____

Peninsula

- A peninsula is a piece of land that is almost surrounded by water.

- It is connected to the mainland by a narrow strip of land.

- Peninsulas can have beaches, cliffs, and forests.

- Peninsulas can have beautiful views of the ocean or sea.

- Some peninsulas are big, and some are small.

- Florida is a famous peninsula in the United States.

- Peninsulas are special places because they are close to the water on three sides.

- People often visit peninsulas for vacations and outdoor activities.

Write 4 facts you have learned.

Peninsula

1. _____

_____

2. _____

_____

3. _____

_____

4. _____

_____

Plain

- Plains are large, flat areas of land.

- They are covered with grass and have few trees.

- Many animals, like bison and prairie dogs, live on plains.

- Plains are good places for farming because the soil is rich.

- Plains can be found on every continent.

- People often raise cattle and other animals on plains.

- Plains can have rivers and streams running through them.

- The Great Plains are a famous plain in North America.

- Plains can be very windy because there are few hills or trees.

Write 4 facts you have learned.

Plain

1. _____

_____

2. _____

_____

3. _____

_____

4. _____

_____

Plateau

- Plateaus are large, flat areas of land that are higher than the land around them.
- They can be formed by volcanic activity or movement of the Earth's crust.
- Plateaus often have steep sides like cliffs.
- Many animals, like antelope and mountain cats, live on plateaus.
- People sometimes farm on plateaus because of the flat land.
- The Colorado Plateau is a famous plateau in the United States.
- The Tibetan Plateau is the highest and largest plateau in the world.

Write 4 facts you have learned.

Plateau

1. _____

_____

2. _____

_____

3. _____

_____

4. _____

_____

Rainforest

- Rainforests are dense forests with lots of rain all year round.

- They are found near the equator in places like the Amazon and Congo.

- Many kinds of plants and animals live in rainforests.

- Animals like monkeys, jaguars, and parrots live in rainforests.

- Rainforests make a lot of the world's oxygen.

- Rainforests are often called the "lungs of the Earth."

- Many medicines come from plants in rainforests.

- Rainforests have different layers: emergent, canopy, understory, and forest floor.

- The Amazon Rainforest is the largest rainforest in the world.

Write 4 facts you have learned.

Rainforest

1. _____

   _____

2. _____

   _____

3. _____

   _____

4. _____

   _____

River

- A river is a large, flowing body of water that moves across the land.
- Rivers usually start in mountains or hills where the snow melts.
- Many animals, like fish, ducks, and beavers, live in rivers.
- People use rivers for drinking water, farming, and transportation.
- Famous rivers include the Nile, the Amazon, and the Mississippi.
- People enjoy activities like fishing, rafting, and kayaking on rivers.
- Rivers often flow into lakes, seas, or oceans at their end.

Write 4 facts you have learned.

River

1. _____

_____

2. _____

_____

3. _____

_____

4. _____

_____

Valley

- Valleys are low areas between mountains or hills.

- Rivers often flow through valleys.

- Valleys can be wide and flat or narrow and steep.

- Many animals, like deer, rabbits, foxes, elk, beavers, raccoons, turkeys, and hawks, live in valleys.

- People often build towns and farms in valleys.

- Valleys have rich soil, which is good for growing crops.

- Valleys are beautiful places with lots of plants and trees.

- There is usually less wind in a valley than on a mountain.

Write 4 facts you have learned.

Valley

1. _____

   _____

2. _____

   _____

3. _____

   _____

4. _____

   _____

Volcano

- A volcano is a mountain that can erupt with lava, ash, and gases.
- Volcanoes form when hot, melted rock called magma rises to the surface.
- When a volcano erupts, it can be very powerful and dangerous.
- The top of a volcano has an opening called a crater.
- Some volcanoes are active and can erupt at any time.
- Other volcanoes are dormant and haven't erupted in a long time.
- Mount St. Helens is a famous volcano that erupted in 1980.
- Volcanoes are found all over the world, especially around the Pacific Ocean.

Write 4 facts you have learned.

Volcano

1. _____

   _____

2. _____

   _____

3. _____

   _____

4. _____

   _____

Wetland

- Wetlands are areas where land is covered by water, often part of the year.
- They can be marshes, swamps, or bogs.
- Wetlands are home to many animals like frogs, turtles, and ducks.
- They provide a home for many fish and birds.
- Plants like cattails and water lilies grow in wetlands.
- Wetlands help clean water by filtering out dirt and pollution.
- Wetlands can help prevent floods by soaking up extra water.
- Some wetlands are salty, and some are freshwater.
- Wetlands are important for the environment to be healthy.

Write 4 facts you have learned.

Wetland

1. _____

   _____

2. _____

   _____

3. _____

   _____

4. _____

   _____

Free Printable Birthday Cards

Would you like to help your child create birthday cards for family members, friends, and teachers?

Get birthday cards with <u>sentence starters</u> and <u>word banks</u>!

Includes:

- 5 designs for students to color
- Sentence starters
- Word banks
- Handwriting lines
- 15 interiors to choose from

Appropriate for all ages.

https://writingstudent.com/pages/birthday-cards-sentence-starters

Check out all the scaffolded writing resources at WritingStudent.com